Oncle

JACQUES TATI

T0000931

Wallace &

NICK P

A Gr
Day

ASTIC
OX

JURASSIC PARK

LE VOYAGE

For "teacher" Sven

I'd like to thank Benjamin d'Aoust, Olivier Thys, and Frédéric Fonteyne for their much-appreciated assistance in my research for this book.

— Chantal Peten
www.chantalpeten.be

Want to Know
a lot to do

Going to the Movies

Written by Florence Ducatteau
Illustrated by Chantal Peten

Clavis

NEW YORK

We're visiting a film studio with our class. Harold and Leila wear special suits with sensors. The cameraperson tells them to paddle as if they're fleeing real danger. Their movements and expressions are captured on film, and all the images are sent to a computer. The computer changes the bodies of the children, but it captures their movements and expressions.

The invention of cinema

Our eyes are fascinating! When we view multiple images at a time, our brains turn them into a film. It's like we're watching 24 images per second!

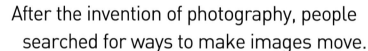

After the invention of photography, people searched for ways to make images move. The result was a camera that could register the rapid succession of images on photosensitive material: film. The images could then be displayed on a screen with a projector. Just like a shadow show or magic lantern, a bright light is flashed onto a white screen. In front of the light, translucent images are magnified on the screen, making it possible for many people to view them at once. Despite many failed attempts, it was successful!

Did you know the people who were watching the movie *The Arrival of a Train at the Station of La Ciotat* (1895) were afraid a real train would squash them?

The movies, from past to present

The invention of the cinema is fairly recent; it's just over one hundred years old. In the beginning, there were only **black and white** images, even though some filmmakers colored their images by hand! Later on, **color film** was invented.

The first movies were **silent films** (films without sound). In the movie theater, a pianist or orchestra played music to highlight the film's most important moments and emotions. Occasionally, in between images, a small sign appeared with an explanation or a dialogue (a conversation between actors). Later on, the **audio tape** was invented, making it possible to hear the dialogues, background sounds, and music.

The Lumière Brothers filmed scenes from daily life. They started with the **documentary cinema**. Georges Méliès invented fantastic stories which incorporated tricks and special effects. He created **fiction film**.

Movie-making techniques are still developing today. Recording is now done digitally, rather than on film. And of course, there are now **3D movies**. When you watch them in the movie theater, you must wear special glasses. What will the movies of the future look like?

Did you know
you can watch thousands of movies in a film museum or a movie library?

Preparing a movie (preproduction)

It all starts with the **director** (the head of the film crew) and their plans for a movie. First, they consider what type of movie they want to make—and what story they want to tell. Then they choose **actors** to tell their story.

Meanwhile, the **executive producer** acquires funding so the film crew, settings, and materials are financially covered. Making a movie is expensive!

The **production manager** searches (sometimes all over the world!) for places (or locations) where the movie can be filmed. When you see a house in a movie, it's possible that the exterior of the house is filmed in an entirely different location than the interior. It's also possible that the interior is filmed in a studio.

The idea behind a movie often comes from the director, or from a book, but it's the **scriptwriter** that writes the story of the film. They divide it into scenes (a scene is a piece of a movie), ensuring that the story has enough tension. The **dialogue writer** writes the dialogues: the words the actors speak to each other.

Then a **storyboard** is made: a series of drawings capturing the director's vision for the film. The storyboard shows the camera angle (perspective) and view (framing). Will the faces of the actors be filmed close-up (from a short distance), or will there be overviews (from a long distance)? Will the camera follow the actors when they move (traveling)? All of these details are included in a storyboard.

close-up:
from a short distance

medium close-up:
from the shoulders up

American shot:
from the thighs up

long shot:
the entire person

overview:
from a long distance

Did you know
there are different film genres?
Adventure, westerns, detective, thriller,
horror, musical, romantic, comedy,
documentary, and so on.

The film crew

Many people are needed to make a movie.

Production and direction

THE ASSISTANT DIRECTOR SUPPORTS THE DIRECTOR WITH ALL THEIR TASKS.

THE EXECUTIVE PRODUCER COLLECTS THE MONEY TO PAY FOR THE SETTINGS, MATERIALS, AND STAFF.

THE DIALOGUE WRITER WRITES THE DIALOGUES OF ALL CHARACTERS.

THE SCRIPT WRITER WRITES THE STORY AND DIVIDES IT INTO SCENES.

THE PRODUCTION MANAGER TAKES CARE OF PRACTICAL MATTERS, LIKE SECURING A FILM LOCATION.

THE DIRECTOR IS THE HEAD OF THE CREW. THEY DECIDE WHAT THE FILM WILL LOOK LIKE AND WHO WILL PLAY EACH ROLE.

THE SCRIPT PERSON ENSURES THAT THERE'S CONSISTENCY, PARTICULARLY WITH COSTUMES AND COSTUME CHANGES.

Settings

THE PROP MANAGER OVERSEES ALL THE OBJECTS THAT ARE NEEDED FOR EACH SCENE.

THE SET DESIGNER DESIGNS THE SETTINGS.

THE SET BUILDER BUILDS THE SETTINGS, INCLUDING ANY FURNITURE THAT CAN'T BE PURCHASED ELSEWHERE.

THE PAINTER PAINTS THE SETTINGS AND FURNITURE.

Camera

THE DIRECTOR OF PHOTOGRAPHY (OR DOP) IS THE HEAD OF THE CAMERA TEAM. THEY DECIDE HOW A SCENE IS SHOT.

THE CAMERAPERSON FILMS THE SCENE.

THE CLAPPER LOADER TELLS THE CAMERAPERSON WHEN THEY CAN START FILMING.

THE GAFFER IS RESPONSIBLE FOR THE LIGHT.

THE PHOTOGRAPHER TAKES PICTURES ON SET (THE PLACE WHERE A SCENE IS BEING FILMED) AND OFF SET.

THE CASTING DIRECTOR ORGANIZES AUDITIONS AND PRESENTS THE ACTORS TO THE DIRECTOR.

THE COSTUME DESIGNER DESIGNS THE CLOTHES THE ACTORS WILL WEAR.

THE STAND-IN PLAYS THE ROLE OF THE LEADING ACTOR DURING DANGEROUS SCENES.

THE HAIRDRESSER TAKES CARE OF THE ACTORS' HAIR AND MAKES WIGS IF NECESSARY.

THE MAKE-UP ARTIST MANAGES THE ACTORS' MAKE-UP, WHICH MIGHT INCLUDE FAKE SKIN (IN HORROR MOVIES, FOR EXAMPLE).

THE LEADING ACTOR PLAYS ONE OF THE LEADING ROLES IN THE MOVIE.

EXTRAS ARE PEOPLE IN MOVIES THAT ARE SEEN AND NOT HEARD. THEY HAVE NO SPEAKING PARTS.

Postproduction

THE COMPOSER COMPOSES OR PLAYS THE MUSIC FOR THE MOVIE.

THE SOUND TECHNICIAN RECORDS THE SOUND. THEY HOLD A MICROPHONE ON A LONG POLE ABOVE THE ACTORS WHEN THEY'RE SPEAKING.

THE EDITOR ARRANGES THE RECORDED SCENES IN A LOGICAL SEQUENCE.

THE FOLEY ARTIST CREATES THE BACKGROUND SOUNDS OF A MOVIE.

THE COLOR CORRECTOR MAKES SURE THE COLORS AND THE BRIGHTNESS OF ALL RECORDED IMAGES ARE CONSISTENT.

THE SOUND EDITOR BRINGS BALANCE TO THE VOICES, BACKGROUND SOUNDS, AND MUSIC.

THE SOUND ENGINEER MANAGES THE SOUND AND ELIMINATES ALL UNWANTED NOISE.

Animation and more

Of course, not every movie uses real people in real places.
There are also animation films and cartoons.

An animation film consists of many different drawings on paper or translucent celluloid.
When you flip through the diverse drawings (24 per second!), an animation develops.
The greater the variety of images, the faster the movement becomes. A cartoon is
often made by more than one illustrator.

Some animation films are made with clay figures or metal robots. The figure is filmed,
the position is slightly changed, the figure is filmed again, and so on. With this
method, it takes a long time to make a movie. Today, digital methods
go much faster. Now we can draw and design characters on
a computer. To make movements look real, motion capture
is used, like with Leila and Harold, when they visited
the studio with their class.

Did you know
the making of a long
animation film requires many
designers and much time?

On set

Some movies are filmed in real landscape settings and buildings. But others are shot in film studios like La Cité du Cinema in Paris or Cinécittà in Rome. Long before the cameras can start rolling, the settings must be built. Other employees take care of the costumes and the make-up.

Special effects have evolved over time. Today, it's possible to create artificial faces that look real! Some are even quite scary!

It's the director's job to guide the actors in their unique roles. In some movies, the emotions of the characters are vital, but in an action movie, the actors are known for their strength and speed. An actor should be able to adapt to every situation: sometimes they get a wooden leg, sometimes a harness, sometimes a monstrous face . . .

Did you know
an actor might spend over four hours getting their makeup done?

Did you know there are cooks on the set who prepare meals for the entire crew during a long day of filming? And of course, the horses have to eat too!

Postproduction

When all scenes have been shot, the editor reviews all "rushes", or bits of film, with the director. The **editor** then arranges them in an appropriate sequence. This process is called **montage**. Rhythm is very important in montage: a film can be slow or fast, calm or suspenseful. Sometimes, special effects are added as well.

If everything is recorded on film, the pieces must be assembled by hand. But today, editing almost always takes place on a computer. Once the editor and director are pleased with the results, the montage is complete.

The **sound editor** collects dialogues, background sounds, and music on audio tape. A foreign movie that plays in our movie theatres will either be subtitled in English or dubbed. That means actors from our country record the English dialog. While they're doing this, the voice actors watch the movie to see how fast they should speak. The English voices replace the foreign ones. Animation movies in particular are often dubbed. It's humorous to hear how voice actors imitate animals . . .

The **foley artist** uses many props to create background sounds: windows, doors, tiles, and parquet floors. Other props might include: broken glass, a stick, a rope, a hot-water bottle, a suitcase with a zipper, footwear, garments, half of a car, water, and sand. The foley artist is even recording the sound of high heels on pavement.

The movie is released

Making a movie often costs a lot of money, but that money can be earned back through movie sales. First, cinemas buy the movie to show it. Then, the movie is distributed on DVD and Blu-ray disks. Finally, the movie is broadcasted on television and streamed on the internet. If a movie is very popular, you might be able to purchase merchandise such as toys, costumes, or books that are related to the movie.

What if you want to go to the movies, but you don't know which movie to choose? You can watch movie trailers (short clips to give you a sense of a movie) or read reviews in the newspaper or on the internet. You can also go to the movie theater and watch how many people are lining up to see a movie. That way, you can see immediately whether the movie is successful or not.

Did you know
a very popular
movie is called
a box-office hit?

Film festivals and movie locations

The American city of movies is Hollywood, where there are countless film studios. The country with the highest number of films produced is India. The Indian film industry is called Bollywood.

Successful actors and actresses can become world-famous stars. Some of them even get a star with their name on it on the pavement of Hollywood Boulevard.

Oscar

Golden Palm

César

Golden Bear

Golden Lion

At film festivals, new movies are shown, and a jury distributes awards to the best films, directors, and actors. The most important movie awards in the United States are the Oscars, or Academy Awards. In Cannes, the best movie receives the Golden Palm. The French movie award is called the César. At the Berlin film festival, one can receive a Golden Bear, and in Venice, a Golden Lion.

Did you know
watching a movie on a big screen in a dark movie theatre feels very different than watching the same movie at home? What do you prefer, and why?

Making movie sounds at home

Leila and her big brother are making background sounds for a movie scene. Their parents are watching the scene on television, but they've muted the sound. Behind the couch, the two children are making background sounds, utilizing various materials. They're also using their voices to dub the dialogues.

You can try it, too! Use anything you like! If you hit the edge of a table with a belt, it sounds like a gunshot. If you tap two plastic cups on the carpet, it sounds like the pounding of hooves. If you pop pellets of paper against the refrigerator door, it sounds like a crackling fire. Flap a leather glove and you hear a bird take off. Experiment with different kinds of surfaces (a wooden floor, a tile floor, a chair or couch) to hear different sounds each time. Knock, scratch, crinkle . . . and listen. If it's helpful, close your eyes.

You can also experiment with different voices. Try talking like a wild bear or a desperate chicken that lost her little ones. Or use the voice of Donald Duck . . .

Make a thaumatrope

A thaumatrope is a disc with a different picture on each side. By turning it very quickly, it appears as if you can see the front and back at the same time.

Consider a picture that consists of two parts, like:

- a goldfish in a bowl
- flowers in a vase
- a man in an outfit
- French fries in a paper cone
- a rocket and its flame

1. Draw two identical circles on a piece of paper and cut them out.

2. Draw one illustration on the first circle and the other illustration on the second. Make sure the placement and sizing are correct.

3. Set the circles on top of each other (not back-to-back!) and hold them in front of a lamp or against a window. Do the images match? (If not, repeat the process and try again.)

4. Affix the backs of the pieces together with glue and a skewer in the middle.

5. Make sure the drawings are upright on the skewer.

6. Test your thaumatrope by rolling the skewer quickly between your hands. If all goes well, you'll see one image!

A very confused script person ...

Here's a scene from an old movie. The story takes place in the first century of our era. The script pers[on] must've been confused, because there are seven mistakes in this scene. Can you find them all?

Mini-quiz

1. How do pictures move in an animation movie?

2. One of the first movies included a fast-moving train. Why was the audience afraid?

3. Have movies always had sound and image?

4. Who's in charge of making movies?

5. What's the role of an executive producer?

6. What are extras?

7. Why must a sound technician be cautious?

8. Who turns individual recordings into a movie?

9. Are the inside and outside of a house always filmed at the same location?

10. What award is given for best movie during the festival of Cannes?

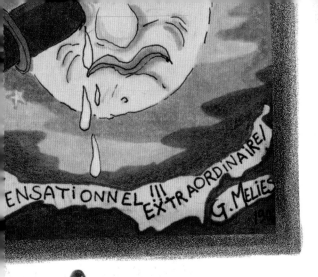

ENSATIONNEL !!! EXTRAORDINAIRE!
G. MELIES
194

E.T.

Steven Spielberg

APLIN
MODERN
TIMES